SUCCESSFUL WAYS TO ACHIEVE SUCCESS

A GUIDE TO SUCCESS

CHETAN DHOLAKIYA

ISBN 979-888555105-2

I dedicated this book to my Respected Mother and My supporter my bestest friend Sujali Sojitra. My parents and I must say My bestest friend who always supports and encourage me just like my parent that all made me so capable that I can make a positive change in someone's life and at the same time faithfully carry out my responsibility.

All I have to say to you is that if this book helps you a little bit to become a successful, then please encourage others to read this book once who really want to be successful, who really need this type of books. I pray to God that you move towards your goal & succeed in your life whatever your goal is.

Contents

CHAPTER I

First Be A Good Human

"It Is A Good Thing To Be A Big Person, But Being A Good Person Is A Big Deal"

For become a successful person you should be first a good person.

Kind, helpful, supportive, understanding, patient and loving are some of the words that come to mind when listing the qualities of a good person. In general, you know that a person is good at what they do

Like flowers in a garden, we're all here to make the world a beautiful place, so bloom with the person to whom you love the most. Today's world is full of selfishness, even relationships have become like this, so why not be different from the world and be who you are instead of what someone else wants you to be?

Life is short and beautiful, so enjoy every moment in every possible manner to the extend of being a child who does not knows what he/she doing... Keep that innocence in your relationship because sometimes we need someone to simply be there and not to fix anything or do anything in a particular, but just to let us feel or know their presence and for being supporting and cared about what we are...

"Be a good person, success follows you automatically"

CHAPTER II

Be Simple But Significant

"A simple style can only be afforded by great minds"

Most of the time, when we talk about a simple lifestyle, we are referring to a combination like humble, down to earth but very competitive and tough.

In most cases, however, simple people are less complicated and more flexible in their lifestyle. They usually avoid being the center of attention, but still remain relevant to their area of expertise. Most of all, practice and persistence reduce our expectations.

A simple person is someone who is able to find happiness in smaller things in life like having a chocolate or a good conversation. He/She is content with what he/she has and tries to make things better for others which not necessarily means he/she is not ambitious.

He/She doesn't have a lot of layers in his personality. He/She does what they commits and sees others also the same way. I guess a simple person wants the basic things in life with lots of love and a couple of caring and similar people around.

"A person can achieve everything if he/she is simple and humble."

Living simple is being down to earth...it doesn't mean to live simply with simple things and ideas... it doesn't include you are rich or poor and full of your needs or lacking your wishes to complete but still thinking for other people... but still caring for others... but still want to play in playgrounds... but still want to eat street foods...

It is not about getting obsessed what you are getting and what you will get... It is about providing your gratitude as a person to other people... Living simple include your idea and point of view for other people and for yourself too... how you treat others and yourself...

It is about getting respect from everyone and giving the same.

"Not Just The Name, But Importance In Someone's Life With Respect That is a Relationship. Otherwise Everything Is A Formality".

It is about letting others without any jealousy between.. Living simple is not that simple but if you understand this simple thing than it will be the simplest thing you ever know!!

CHAPTER III

Essential Mindset Needed To Be Successful

Having the right mindset is very crucial when you are on the path to success. So let me show you how to change your mindset for a successful life...

1. Think Positive:

Changing my mindset started with starting my day right and always thinking positively even though I was having a bad day. Always look on the bright side of your situation. Now, it can be a little hard for us when maybe we fail in school, get depressed, or whatever you think is wrong in your life. This is why positive thinking can change your whole life.

Every time you wake up in the morning, be sure to thank God for a new day and say how great your day will be.

Waking up every day is such a blessing. You know that God is waking you up because you still have a goal to accomplish. Even if things aren't going so well, be positive. Negativity will not improve your situation.

2. Gratitude:

Gratitude is a must when you are on a journey to change your mind and achieve success. Being grateful for what I already have motivates me to work hard for an even better lifestyle. For example, being grateful for: waking up every day, fresh air, a roof over my head and much more, for which I can be grateful or Say you want a new smartphone because the current one is not working, or you just want to upgrade, make sure you are grateful for the one you already have and clean it when it is dirty. The current smartphone is the new one you want and you treat it just like you would treat the new one. These simple acts are so crucial in changing your mindset and practicing gratitude.

Gratitude erases negativity. When you are having a bad day and negativity shows up, remember to be content with whatever you already have in life.

3. Believe in Yourself:

Believing in yourself is the most important thing if you are on your path to success.

As simple as it sounds, it was pretty difficult for me. I wanted to believe that I could publish my own book.

I just started writing, but I took the first step, I believed in myself. So if you are looking to start your own business, don't doubt yourself or reconsider the situation, just take the first step.

How will you be successful when you doubt yourself?

The answer is you **can't.**

And let's say you believe in yourself, but there is still a bit of doubt somewhere in your head. You wonder, but what if I fail, what if I'm not good enough, what if people don't like my idea, and the list goes on. These questions and whether they stopped me from writing in future. I was always busy rethinking the situation. Don't make the same mistake.

So do it whenever you want, let's start a business or whatever you want to do. When these questions come up, close them and remember that you believe in your ability and ability to achieve your goals. Write down your goals and remind yourself or read them aloud each day that you can and will achieve them.

BUT not only believe, work to achieve them. Scrolling social media all day won't help.

CHAPTER IV

Enhance Your Value

A concise message has great power, so I have selected three quick tips that can help you increase your worth through the continued application of the Compensation Law:

1. Educated Yourself Continuously:

Whenever possible, you should strive to learn more about your field, but you should also find time to learn about other things. For Example: Related fields, Subjects that interest you, Influential people of the present or the past.

2. Encourage Others:

Instead of focusing on realizing the mistakes of others, which is less effective for lasting change, discover others doing the right thing and focus on the accomplishments of those around you. This includes your co-workers, supervisors, subordinates, friends and family Members.

In the workplace, this approach has a positive impact: when you encourage and give credit to your teammates.

3. Create a Job Vision:

Having a clear overview of the job will help you take a broader view of your role, your behavior, and the improvements you could make on a more sophisticated level. It often helps you to review how your boss might see your position.

Taking a less myopic perspective can also help you reflect on new ways in which you can contribute, thereby adding value to the company.

To increase your value, you must first gain confidence in yourself, and change your mindset. Always keep in mind that what matters is what you want to get out of the experience. Don't put any unnecessary pressure on yourself and consider every act you do in accordance with your vision as a way to increase your worth

CHAPTER V

How Can I Become Rich?

'The Psychology of Money' by Morgan Housel, I came across a very interesting sentence, '**THE HIGHEST FORM of wealth is the ability to wake up every morning and say, "I can do whatever I want today."**

You are not rich because you have millions or billions in your bank account. You are not rich because you live in a big house, drive an expensive car or own a private jet, or have dozens of servants cooking your food and cleaning your house.

You get rich when you can do what you want and live your life your own way. We want money because money gives us the ability to do what we want, when we want, with whom we want, and for as long as we want. Unfortunately, money, which is only a means to happiness, becomes an end in itself for most people.

In fact, most people are so obsessed with money that they sacrifice their time, relationships, health, and even happiness to make money. If you can able to several billions by sacrificing all you have, you are not rich but the poorest man in the world.

You get rich when you have enough money to meet your daily needs for the future and enough time to live your life on your terms and do the things you love to do.

You can have enough money in two ways.

1. Increase your income so much that you can fulfill all of your desires.

2. Reduce your needs to the point that you can create excess within existing income and have enough savings in a short period of time to have enough money in your account to meet all of your needs

Most individuals follow the primary approach and never feel wealthy enough. Wise people follow the second approach and that they forever feel rich enough to measure their life fully.

CHAPTER VI

How to boost your self-confidence

To develop a positive self-image, you have to reflect on your self-perception, and develop healthy habits that will help you do so.

Don't compare yourself to others:

Whether you're comparing your looks to your friends on Facebook or comparing your salary to your friend's income, comparisons are not healthy. In fact, a 2020 study published in Personality and Individual Differences found a direct link between envy and your attitude towards yourself. Researchers found that people who compared themselves to others felt envious, and the more envy they felt, the worse they felt themselves.

Make Sure You Look Good:

It is important to take care of your appearance. Shower and shave regularly without getting upset about it; Make time every day to be presentable to the world. These simple little actions can have a dramatic effect on your self-confidence.

Create a positive self-image:

Creating a positive view of yourself often begins with adjusting your thinking and limiting comparisons with others.Start building positive self-image by introducing yourself as who you want to be. For example, imagine him in the position you're interviewing for with reliable skills.

Once you have established a positive self-image, consider participating in self-affirmation activities. Self-affirmation involves making positive, uplifting statements about yourself to question any negative thoughts you may have.

Make sure you surround yourself with positive people:

Notice how your friends feel about you. Do your friends make you up or down? Do they constantly judge you or do they accept you for who you are?

The people you hang out with influence their thoughts and attitudes about you more than you think. If after a date with a certain person you feel bad about yourself, it may be time to say goodbye.

Identify your skills, strengths, and talents:

Those who lack self-confidence tend to focus on their weaknesses and flaws and obsess over them. One way to improve your self-image is to spend time figuring out how God gave you gifts.

- What are you good at?
- What did you do successfully?
- In which subjects were you successful at school?
- In what did people tell you that you were good?

Your Uniqueness Is What Makes You Special:

Too many people complain about what they are not, wanting to be someone else, wanting a better personality, more fun, or more business skills.

Instead, take the time to be thankful for who you are. They have many admirable qualities and you should take the time to focus on them instead of who you want to be.

CHAPTER VII

Growing a Growth Mindset

A growth mindset is a concept that is developed and promoted in Carol Dweck's book Mindset: The New Psychology of Success. By the way, this book can have a life-changing impact if you read it and then practice the ideas you've read each time.

The concept of mindset in general is defined as the attitude and belief that we have about the world around us, the people we interact with, and ultimately about ourselves. Carol Dweck suggests that the vision we have of ourselves can drastically affect the way we lead. our life She distinguishes between two mentalities that people generally have:

- **A fixed mindset:** the belief that our skills, strengths, and qualities are set in stone and there is nothing we can do to change them for better or for worse.

- **A Growth Mindset** - Believing that we can develop the same skills and qualities through commitment and long-term effort.

While a fixed mindset builds up over time by listening to messages from an early age about what we can, should and shouldn't do (usually from parents, relatives, teachers), a growth mentality is mainly encouraged by ourselves when we consciously choose learning opportunities from which we can benefit.

Why growth mindset is so important?

Simply put, the mindset that you acquire throughout your life can help you grow. There is a huge difference between the two mindsets and how much they can add strength or affect your personal growth. a look at everyone.

Fixed mindset:

- **Having a fixed mindset means:** You believe that your qualities are set in stone, that you can only have a certain level of intelligence, personality type, or moral character.
- **Nurturing by family and teachers:** They have often heard statements like: "You are so clever!" or "You are a genius!" or "You are natural!" during your childhood.
- **How that mindset is reflected in your life today:** You think you are only good at pursuing intellectual endeavors, but you are really bad at athletics (or vice versa); or that you are excellent at math and accounting but are having a hard time learning a new language.

Growth mindset:

- **Having a growth mindset means:** You believe that through conscious and continuous effort you can develop your qualities and change and grow with your life experiences.
- **Nurturing by family and teachers:** They heard statements like: "You worked so hard and that's why you passed the exam!" or "You had a difficult time in this class at the beginning of the year, but you wanted to learn more and are very good at it now!" during your childhood.
- **How that mindset is reflected in your life today:** Even if you struggled with math class in elementary school, you want to get a business degree that requires math skills and you're not letting your previous experience hold you back from his title.

CHAPTER VIII

Learn To Speak Less And Observe More

First, remember that listening is a more important part of a conversation. I'm going to give you a few reasons why you really appreciate listening.

Think of it in this way. When you speak, you can only say what you already know and keep repeating what you already know. Instead, when you are listening you are listening to something new, something which you do not already know. Even if you know it, you are hearing it in a different perspective in a new way so you are learning more that way. Give your words something valuable, if you speak less, they will listen to you more and you will waste your precious energy in more speaking. So make sure it counts when you speak.

Listening takes less energy but requires patience. Be patient to listen to him with a smile, respect all perspectives and arguments. If you respect the arguments put forward, you will get the same for your points of view. It is wise to listen to opinions you disagree with with the same respect and consideration. It increases your credibility and creates an unbiased picture of you.

Also asking a questions (asking the right questions) to the person in front of you is a more effective way of proving your point (in a debate). that is why, lawyers tend to ask more questions and the other person speaks in turn. to prove his point.

Suppose a person is lying or something and you know the other person is lying. You know some of facts which can prove you right. Instead of shouting "you are lying and putting your facts out loudly", you give him a chance to speak and ask them detailed questions. He will get nervous while telling in detail and then you put your facts out...he will be caught.

CHAPTER IX

Remember To Always Dream Big

Aim for the moon and you may land among the stars.... dreaming huge will take you off from you expetations... therefore the trick is to lower the expetations and dream big.

Don't let a thought cross your mind where you are today as you decide where you are going. We all have the right to do anything that makes us happy, and that includes dreaming big.

Everyone can dream big. The question is, are you making any specific efforts to make this happen?

Get clarity about what your dream is, why you want it, then make ONE decision to devote yourself to a dream and make it your goal.

Once you commit, burn the ships, burn the bridge, and pursue them with determination. Sure, simple, direct, like an arrow to the target.

The path will surely have ups and downs, but never mind because once you have made the final decision and have your determination to make your dream come true at all costs, you will achieve it. And if you don't massively implement your dream, it just means that your dream is not that important to you. So turn around and dedicate yourself to what is really important to you.

Many people are afraid of dreaming too much because they feel that all hope is lost when they cannot achieve it, but the trick is that all hope is never lost and will achieve any dream / goal with the right attitude can be. It all starts with yourself.

Tell yourself that you will improve to achieve this goal and that you will do anything to achieve it. Think about the necessary and desired steps that need to be taken to get closer to your goal. It gives you something to do, but it will also give you something to look forward to.

Dream as big as you want and once you do it you'll be glad you pursued it in the first place.

CHAPTER X

Signs of Rich People

It is a common misconception that wealthy people spend money anytime, anywhere; not true at all; In fact, they're pretty calculating when it comes to spending money on amenities and luxuries, and that's what keeps their financial position intact. They have a structured and organized lifestyle and refrain from buying things that do not have great value.

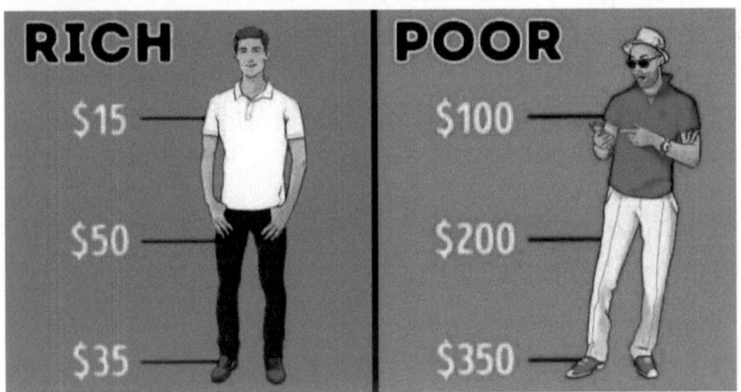

The expensive things looks attractive enough, don't buy it. Many may not know, but without planning buying is one reason your bank balance hits your balance low.

You'll be surprised how much all of your digital TV channels and OTT platform subscriptions add up. Rich people rarely sit in front of the TV and prefer to have a good digital subscription to enjoy casual entertainment anytime. So think twice before you renewing the pack.

It is hard to believe that wealthy people do not buy luxurious items for their daily lifestyle. Buying fancy clothes, bags, shoes, or expensive cars may look promising, but it can quickly affect your bank statement. Buying a luxury item once or twice is fine, but don't end up buying things that you don't really need.

Wealthy people don't waste their money buying the latest digital gadgets or go on crazy expensive vacations, but prefer to make themselves comfortable on their existing phone or in a cozy and comfortable hotel. It is advisable to spend only certain amount on things that are important in the long run.

Investing in over budget home that is not a smart thing. You should look for deals that involve a lot of negotiation so that you can afford them. Showing off the big house and in that additional renovations and interiors will also rip you off completely.

CHAPTER XI

Trying To Impress Others Is A Waste Of Time

If you've been trying to impress others for a long time, it may have become your habit, either a good habit or a bad habit, these repetitive actions are trapped in our brain and, after that it become a habitual in routine process.

What can be stop this bad habit?

Whenever you're pursuing a goal or completing a task, check its validity by asking a question, "Did I choose it to impress others or is it on my priority list?" In the first case, replace the task with the priority that you really want to get done.

Breaking a habit requires constant attention to your actions. Whatever you do, watch your intentions behind your actions. Each time you complete a task, you have to change your priorities if you want to impress others. You will soon notice the difference. It's perfectly fine to stop watching or being distracted to pay attention to your intentions initially, but keep trying.As you already know, failed attempts are the stairs to a successful attempt.

Never let yourself be determined by the opinions of others. Opinions are not facts. People will call you crazy, ugly, fat, and any other name, so never let people's opinions rule you.

As long as you keep your head in the right place, it really matters.If people want to tell their story the way they want it, even if it's not real, then leave it and that's perfectly fine because it's the world they live in and that gives them comfort, so let her. I'm not saying you have to put it up with it, but most of the world, even those who say they are "real", aren't, so remember that it's your life, your choices, your consequences. Focus on keeping your head in right place.

"Impressing others is a good thing, but not impressing others by being someone who you are not. Instead of that impressing by being who you are."

CHAPTER XII

Learn From Everyone, But Don't Follow Anyone

It is the same message that has been repeated numerous times in every age. While we must learn from what the world has to offer, we must strive to make something better of it. Or we would just repeat what others have already done, follow the herd and never let our own individuality shine. The world could be less rich than if we let our own light shine.

"You are an original, don't take your place as a copy."

What is the use of becoming someone's carbon copy ?

There is a reason even twins are different.

First, we need to understand that learning and following are two different things. Most of us, while learning from someone, will automatically begin to act like the person we are learning from. We will begin to put ourselves in their shoes and try to solve problems in our lives. .

We should not follow their methods to solve our life problems. Because the problems and situations forced by them would be much different from ours (not most of the times). We should act and solve problem based on the situation we are dealing with.

Basically, we should learn from everyone, but not follow anyone blindly. Let Your Bliss Lead You.

CHAPTER XIII

Improve Your Argument Instead of Raising Your Voice

First, overcome your anger. Trying to have a discussion, or argument, while one or both parties are angry is a pointless exercise. When emotions run high, people tend not to really listen to what is being said. Let your own emotions control your words and actions. So learn to collect yourself and let go of your anger, or take the time to calm down and ask them to continue the conversation with you later.

I prefer the term discussion because arguments look more like a fight in which both sides are trying to "win". There is seldom openness or space for both sides to see each other's point of view. So if the goal is to win and lose the other person, then I would say that the motivation behind your argument is petty and childish.

However if the goal to to have the other person see your view point, to recognize it's validity and to come to some sort of mutual agreement, then have a discussion. Of course the requirement for a discussion is that both sides keep open minds and truly listen to one another. You must be willing to accept the possibility that either, or both sides will have a changing their mind. Conversely, neither party could change their position and when as long as they understand each other's views and why they are defending them, maybe something good will come out of it.

Instead of trying to win an argument, try to have a discussion with a win-win outcome.

CHAPTER XIV

Key Highlights

- ***It Is A Good Thing To Be A Big Person, But Being A Good Person Is A Big Deal.***

- ***For become a successful person you should be first a good person.***

- ***Be a good person, success follows you automatically.***

- ***A simple style can only be afforded by great minds.***

- ***A person can achieve everything if he/she is simple and humble.***

- ***Not Just The Name, But Importance In Someone's Life With Respect That is a Relationship. Otherwise Everything Is A Formality.***

-

Believing in yourself is the most important thing if you are on your path to success.

•

THE HIGHEST FORM of wealth is the ability to wake up every morning and say, "I can do whatever I want today."

•

Aim for the moon and you may land among the stars. Dream as big as you want and once you do it you'll be glad you pursued it in the first place.

•

Don't waste your time to look rich.

•

Impressing others is a good thing, but not impressing others by being someone who you are not. Instead of that impressing by being who you are.

•

You are an original, don't take your place as a copy. We should learn from everyone, but not follow anyone blindly. Let Your Bliss Lead You.

•

Instead of trying to win an argument, try to have a discussion with a win-win outcome.

9 798885 551052

Printed by Libri Plureos GmbH in Hamburg, Germany